Wild Kingdom

Wild Kingdom

POEMS BY

Vijay Seshadri

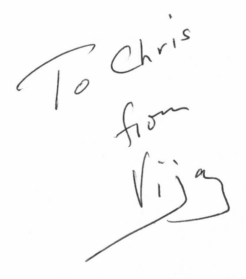

GRAYWOLF PRESS

Publication of this volume is made possible in part by a grant provided
by the Minnesota State Arts Board through an appropriation by the
Minnesota State Legislature, and by a grant from the National Endowment
for the Arts. Significant additional support has been provided by the
Andrew W. Mellon Foundation, the Lila Wallace-Reader's Digest Fund,
the McKnight Foundation, and other generous contributions from
foundations, corporations, and individuals. Graywolf Press is a member
agency of United Arts, Saint Paul. To these organizations and individuals
who make our work possible, we offer heartfelt thanks.

Published by Graywolf Press
2402 University Avenue, Suite 203
Saint Paul, Minnesota 55114

Printed in the United States of America.

ISBN 978-1-55597-236-3

4 6 8 9 7 5 3

Library of Congress Catalog Card Number: 95-80895

Grateful acknowledgment is made to the following publications in which some of the poems in this book have previously appeared.

AGNI:
"The Refugee," "Beginner," "The Testimonies of Ramon Fernandez"

Antaeus:
"Made in the Tropics"

Boulevard:
"Prothalamion"

The Nation:
"A Sketch from the Campaign in the North"

The New Yorker:
"Elegy," "Divination in the Park," "The Reappeared,"
"Locus Solus," "Alien Nation"

The Paris Review:
"Lifeline" (recipient of 1995 Bernard F. Conners Long Poem Prize)

Shenandoah:
"'Too Deep to Clear Them Away,'" "This Fast-Paced, Brutal Thriller,"
"My Esmeralda"

The Southwest Review:
"The Lump"

The Threepenny Review:
"from An Oral History of Migration," "A Werewolf in Brooklyn,"
"Street Scene"

Western Humanities Review:
"Party Girl"

"My Esmeralda," "This Fast-Paced, Brutal Thriller," "Made in the Tropics,"
and "A Sketch from the Campaign in the North" were also reprinted in the
anthology, *Under 35: The New Generation of American Poets*, Ed. Nicholas
Christopher (Anchor Books, 1989).

The author would like to thank Alice Quinn for her support
and encouragement, and would also like to thank the
New York Foundation for the Arts for its generous financial assistance.

Contents

For my mother and father

1

Made in the Tropics

Bobby Culture ("Full of Roots and Culture")
and Ranking Joe ("Man Make You Widdle
Pon Your Toe") shift down
in the gloaming, snap off
their helmets, kill their engines, park
one thousand cubic centimeters
of steeled precision Japanese art.
Their bands drive up
in fur-trimmed vans, unload and unwrap
the hundred-watt speakers, thousand-watt amps,
mikes and mike stands,
guitars, cymbals, steel cans,
at the Blue Room Lawn on Gun Hill Road
by the Bronx botanical gardens.
The sun over Jersey
kicks and drops
into the next of its ready-made slots,
and, like a dark lotion
from a pitcher poured, night fills
the concrete hollows, and the grass
cools in the projects,
the glowing lakes contract
around their artificial islands,
the gardens breathe
easier in the dwindling fever
of today's unbearable summer.
They say the tropics
are moving north,
the skullcap of ice melting
from both the pole now pointed
toward the sun
and the one pointing away.
But what they say is hardly heard here,
where the cooling brickwork
engine red Edwardian

railroad flats empty
their tenants, who gather
in twos and threes, float down
from the stations,
and congregate at the Blue Room Lawn
to celebrate Independence
Day in Jamaica.
The bass line fires up.
From Savanna-La-Mar to Gun Hill Road
the backwash of reggae spirals
to its perch, ripples
and flares its solar wings
along the upended moving limbs,
as if a chain were passed through every wrist,
as if a chain were tied from hip to hip.
The sun does what it does because the earth tilts.

Street Scene

The job of redemption, with its angels and lawyers,
runs late into the morning;
the halls are empty, and from sea green foyers
where aquamarine jackets sag unused
no one walks out to be disabused
by the day, so confident and businesslike.
The domiciled, stunned, paralyzed, in mourning

for the vanishing illuminations, radium-edged,
that made their nerve ends glow
in the dark, are secretly pledged
to attenuate themselves in this,
the spirit's nocturnal crisis,
and still twitch with dreamwork,
and won't open their eyes. But although

not enough energy otherwise subsists
for the nurse to pop an antihistamine
and rise from her viral mists,
for the existential tough guy and thief
to wake up to some extra grief,
for the dog to be led to the park,
for the *viejo* to paint his fire escape green,

so that their race might never be caused to perish
from the contradictions of flight,
up above the satellite dish
pigeons of every color but exactly one size
mob, scatter, and reorganize
to practice crash landings on the street
that divides the black neighborhood from the white.

And at a distance rinsed of charity and malice,
their riots are being umpired by
the unmentionable, porticoed phallus
of the Williamsburgh Savings Bank clock tower,
which manufactures the next hour,
serene in an ongoing function
it can never be called on to abjure or justify.

Divination in the Park

1.

Under the bursting dogwoods, et cetera,
having just finished a pear for lunch,
I lie over the earth, to feel it swim
inside my posture, and sleep,

while full-bellied women pole home with small children,
and black waves fling
grappling hooks and grab by inches
the torn-off, uplifted rocks

stranded offshore like apple trees in the fog.

2.

The upper parts of the earth are slowly thawing.
Less than slowly, the groundwater
rises in the crevices and exposed places,
five strata down where the fossils are.

The winter was mild. In the bulbs and empty hives
spring rubs the velvet from its new brace of horn,
and around the drowning rocks
the feral light of equinox

sheds a pattern on the ocean.

3.

To think that before today, of all the days,
I was less than a snake sunning on a rock,
but that now I'm
the lord of the serpents in the temple,

worshipped and adorned in my eloquent lengths.
So what if I fail the test of time?
I cling to the earth as it banks and glides.
Miners enter my abandoned skin

with strings of lights and diagrams.
Gods on couches ring the horizon.

"Too Deep to Clear Them Away"

A woman is calling my phone for Paul.
No Paul here, lady.
No Paul, no John, no Arturo, just me
and fir and alder stumps
that stretch out like a half-buried battalion
from the ridge spine furrowed
by the wheel tracks of the yarder. Men
come here to cut and haul,
but what they cut grows on.

She calls again. No Paul, lady. Pablo!
He must have gone back to the island. Give
him up. A man lives here awhile and then
another man comes and takes his number.
And across the gutted valley under
next year's stand of sacrificial timber
the split-tongued fir cones plan
vengeance from their beds of moss.

No, I don't want to go to a movie.
I want to sit on my stump and read,
and plot, and imagine things. How,
for example, as night comes on and, grown
tired of the tunes from the buildings,
one lone window washer hangs his harness on the moon.

The Reappeared

Long after we stopped remembering, word of him
drifts back from the coast
to let us know he's still hanging on

in someone else's place and time,
living in a shed in their ivy-choked gardens—
his head shaved, his altered face,

the skin in patches under his eyes.
Supposedly, though, he's still tender and wise;
and having found out it's the same there as here—

the heat breaking out of its sack,
the stars wobbling on their black thrones—
he's made up his mind never to come back.

It's all the same; and on its verge
the borderless ocean scrawls and scrawls
reiterations which repeat

that it's all the same,
and he can fall into it and never change—
resurface, and simply swim away.

Elegy

The ambulance is gone. The squall's
ragged edge fingers
the fresh green stitchings on the alder trees.
Its belly cracks open and pours

through the timbered swale in back of the house
where, with the lights lit early,
the dangerous hours

of a slowly imploding
spring evening circle
the person left behind to answer the calls.

Friend, you're in the hands of professionals now —
shaved and scoured,
black life mask strapped to your mouth,

ampules of glycerin, plasma
by the quart, blossoming in the branches
of your temporary yard, your eyes
reflecting the oscillating lines —

and your heart's plush chambers fibrillate,
in distention darken and swell
three times their size,

swelling in one perpendicular
effort until they
collapse at last.
Friend, it grieves me that you're breaking

your promise to take me hunting.
This fall, you said, on opening day,
when the alders

are nervous with change,
you'd come to my door and we'd drive
the Upper Bay Road to the blind.

The Refugee

He feels himself at his mind's borders moving
down the fifteen rows of laid-out soil
and out to the fence where the mulch heaps spoil
beside the rust-scabbed, dismantled swing
and the visions that disturb him sometimes spring
up from a harmless garden-hose coil:
the jackbooted armies dripping spoors of oil
that slick the leaf and crap the wing. . . .

He sees each rifle as we who see him,
in the crystal blizzard of a century's static,
try to reach him with our two-bit magic.
But he escapes us to roam in the garden:
too clear to look through or distant to ask;
pinned like a flower on the genocidal past.

A Sketch from the Campaign in the North

Just before dawn the women are washing
skirts and blouses, slacks from Hong Kong,
scrubbing their cotton on pockmarked boulders,
cleaning their limbs with mud and lemons
along the turbid river.
At the edge of the jungle, in surplus tents,
the men are talking without weakness or strength
of the recent change in the government.
On the other bank the soldiers are waiting
for the sun to rise from the hills behind them,
not smoking, not talking, in place and unmoving
as the leaves above them waver.
The day unfolds as if kept in a folder
on a desk in the capital.
The sun rises and blinds the river
the soldiers line up and fire from its cover
the air is gravid with sulfur
the river takes blood without changing color
a siren signals the end of the hour
and later in the capital
word is leaked to the foreign papers—
not even their souls climbed free to safety.
There are no handholds up that wall of light.

Of and Relating To

Last week every single night was absent,
leaving an impenetrable blank,
with its smoke from burning tires
and the weak, pestilential grinding of trucks;

but tonight has gone by with a will of its own—
exfoliating, extreme
in its intricacy—
like a drowned field seen from the window

of a commuter express,
brimming with the silver of yesterday's flood,
grazed by the languid,
trailing leg

of the heron, thick with cutthroats
and newly sprung minnows
who act as if they know
how they got there.

They watch the truants, knee-deep
in the muck, and studiously avoid
the well-aimed rocks and the hooks
baited with dough balls,

and scrutinize the witch carried down in a litter
to hand out oranges and kiss off
the herons. She lets
the minnows go unnoticed.

The moon sets, flushed and fully repentant,
its two halves finally joined;
and a night that didn't
fall short of what it professed

is finally reinterred, bequeathing
several unrecognizable objects —
three peaches and a spirit lamp
scattered on the window's sunlit ledge.

The Testimonies of Ramon Fernandez

I don't want to back in and pretend it's wrong anymore—
I know it's right
to put the pedal to my appetite
until I hear the engine roar.
Alone inside my six hundred muscles,
almost personless
in an accelerating cubbyhole,
I can scale the metalled roadways
a co-conspirator of those
for whom the green lights synchronize
and are, in fact, made.
Has anyone ever said about them
they spin their wheels,
grind the vicious circle,
or go out of their way to entertain
ideas once fresh now slippery with blood?
Of course not.
And just looking at me
you can see I should be running with them.
I really should.
But that day I found a devil more subtle,
who offered me from his split mountain
not the kingdoms of earth,
with mule trains, janissaries,
merchant princes,
but fifteen acres on the Alsea River
where the road to Corvallis turns
up to the ridges
only part ruined
by the yarder and the backhoe,
and the woods hoard twilight
long after the sun
bends its attentions to Oriental nations,
leaving a mind long unreconciled dazzled
in that pure half-darkness

as it hears
the simple running of those supple waters.
Believe me when I tell you
what I stand accused of now
I would have done for much less
than that. But there was more:
Terry and Jane stood by the cistern.
The years since I'd seen them —
listless, oneiric,
walking invisible through the burning city —
the conspiracy of error, event,
and defective mythologies
that had cut me out
to be sent to the block
the way a good dingo cuts a lamb from the flock,
fell away and dissolved.
Substance stopped being visible,
or even visual,
and then I imagined that the sun
had come back, reflected
in the enormous mirror
through which the handiwork of its aeons
had continuously passed,
but so close I could abide
its gaze, and even see myself
on or about its giant acreage
of plasma no human
can seriously admonish, under
the perfection yellow
plasmic hurricanes
that deteriorate inwardly
in a process whereby
the subatomic realm is fused
with that which contains elephants,
elected officials, smart bombs,
periwinkles, cherry esplanades,
and the law of the excluded middle.
Did I give in, you ask? Did I submit
to the purity of that vision?

Is the Pope Catholic?
Tired a little of gawking
at my sudden wealth,
I turned back down to the river.
A 58-faceted diamond, blasted
from Transvaal kimberlite,
smuggled out in a miner's
large intestine, cut and polished
in an Amsterdam cellar, and stolen
from a window display
on 47th Street,
could show us no more of what we actually crave
when it comes to fire
than the water rising at my feet
and shimmering backwards
to the hundreds of tributaries,
shaping and molding this piece of the Coast Range,
which could easily have been,
according to our atmospheric sciences,
the water of the Amazon
itself, draining more of it
in a single day
that a city of twelve million
drinks in a decade.
Terry and Jane were long gone by now,
but far upstream
on a crimson bed of spawning gravel a hen salmon
dug herself in and nested
as a buck circled in the current above her.
The moon was in phase.
The mouth of the river was crowded
with urchins, kelp forests,
and rockbound stars.
The river began to levitate.
When I finally made up my mind to go
it was floating three feet above
its prelapsarian ditch.
You can shoot me if I'm lying.
Exquisite pain,

permanent sequestration in a black box
four-by-four-by-eight,
and even the "maximum
punishment the law allows"
would be too good for me if one word
of what I've said isn't true
and doesn't constitute the force behind
the actions for which I stand here now.
I can see by your faces that
your hearts are good, and like to think
mine is, too. Believe me then,
acquit me, stand back, and let me work
there, at the water's edge,
which, as it turns out, is also
the edge of sleep.

My Esmeralda

for S.O.K.

Some people like each other and are therefore like each other,
but I like you and therefore I'm
so original a burden on my time
that all the lifeguards ring their bells
when I rise from my exclusive underneath
to wash in your England of seaside hotels,

climb my perch and send off, over the panorama
of what's most yours—those glowing herds
of prehistoric bison, sunk in clear light
up to the eyes, browsing elsewhere
extinct sky-high ferns—
my messenger birds,
speckled and superfine,
to soar the asymptotic line
that touches you at infinity. Big Mama!

Not once in any of the meretricious annals
I'm forced to read have I read
of you, nor through the maps
I have to make sense of
have I ever watched you pass.
Among words, you're the meaning of "glass,"
and you as a river will cut your own channels.

2

Alien Nation

I think I'm around the wrong people today.
Though I know their cousins (who say I'm nice),
veiling their faces they tiptoe away—
some impassive, some afraid,
and others grumbling that they'd
sooner fillet me than talk to me twice.

And look! In the wind that blows where it lists,
their gun ports blazing wide open,
sail phrenic experts and therapists,
miracle workers, psyche massagers,
waving their hand-sewn Jolly Rogers.
All merciful, unthinking (but compassionate) One,

what on earth, exactly, provoked You to melt
the blanket of snow that pacified
the scrofulations of this blistering veldt
with a cold as keen and sweet
to the tongue as the coconut's meat
and made it strange enough to walk inside?

This Fast-Paced, Brutal Thriller

There's always a killer with a name like Tony,
a tie-dyed shirt, and a certain
sad history of deprivation:
just so much evil to get the plot going

down the edge of a formula
nickel-and-dimed
by years of repetition.
There's always an ocean near Hawaii or California

where the detective ponders the copy of a psalm
he once gave in commemoration
to his friend, the victim
(they shared a tin hut in Vietnam),

over whose body the salt water swarms.
Something as strange and uncanny
as Taiwanese packing twine
has been wrapped around the legs and blue arms,

giving the detective, for his deduction, a sign
that the script changed tongues
in the middle of a scene,
and only he's left to render this line

to the bored, puzzled girl on whom the camera can't focus
because she stepped over for a look
from another channel.
She stares right past him as she says, "Jesus,

this show, it's the pits."
And the faces start blending
on the molten screen:
screen before which the defeated imagination sits.

Locus Solus

Though they work hard to illuminate the path for us
that leads to what's such fun to call
our lonely task—ingesting, evacuating, or
coming around furious
to the justice of it all—

the unshriven but discreet, almost transcendental
intercessors of deep space—red
giants, white dwarfs, globular
clusters hanging in the cosmic vineyard—
find their rays deflected by

the arsonist panting on the rug,
the junior partner planting a bug,
the beautifully upholstered mug-

ger rekindling in front of a mirror,
the vigilante flying off to Venice
for two quick sets of tennis
at the Pro-Am Celebrity Tournament there.

Strange luck, and even worse timing:
being here and tossed on the beach,
bareheaded, barefooted, shanghaied
into feeling the climbing

elastic discomfort brought on by a universe
that we now know recoils from us, retreats
and leaves us to lurk
and grope our spongy floors,
who might as well imagine ourselves
wading the shoals at some astral Dunkirk,

so irremediably has a failure of policy and honor
stranded us between (a)
the scorched wheatfields behind us,
and (b) the burning straits ahead. No wonder
nothing shines on me as I push my cat away,

scatter my clippings, and go get my mail —
the selfsame, unsolicited communication
that arrives each morning without fail
and always reads:

"Such as were caught by the undertow
perished smilingly. The rest, of course, you know
from the particulars of our previous letter."

A Werewolf in Brooklyn

Still almost blind in his thinking eye,
the last of the moon, as it zeros in
on the preordained spot, to modify
his downside structures and curry his skin

with its lucent brush, so the dog flares up,
he only can grasp as a metaphor.
A lozenge dissolves in a silver cup
out of which such emptinesses pour

to prove for him the Buddhists right
who say that wolfpacks of nothingness stalk
the signature stinks and blood trails of man,

but that to race with them and let them bite
will do for him much better than
Ping-Pong, kind visitors, electroshock.

The Language War

Inside the friend whose pride I injured
both one day last fall and the summer before,
the impulse thickens to even the score.
He visits my dreams, but won't say a word,

while his double bodies forth, delivered
from guilt, from doubt, and whispers together
with my victims — ex-lovers, my mother —
and pulls my hair and shouts. Hasn't he heard

yet, the jerk, that the Wall is down for good,
the Rock unrolled; that people strive to live
again, speak up, and are misunderstood;

that pen pals meet; that nations slip their fetters?
Obviously not: he won't answer my letters.
His ink is frozen, and he can't forgive.

Little Treasury of Best-Loved Lines

"One might have thought of sight
but who could think of what it sees. . . ."
Did Francis Parkman say that first,
or Bishop Pike, or Maimonides,

pulled down from his palfrey
on the flight out of Spain?
Exhausting as the effort is
to sit in the dust and unskein

these impossibly tangled legacies
of poets and whatnots, half-remembered,
strung out over an inscape
of graven images and dismembered

statues, "where all the ladders start"—
worse than a horror show—
the hand still perforates time
to panhandle the wise, because they do know

the score, and can sing it out
with feeling. The divine afflatus,
in full spate in their brains,
justifies their priestly status

as our uncorrupted protectors
and counterweights to power, who are
gems in the respective epochs
of Timur, Dionysus, FDR,

and the Council of Twenty-three.
And the insights accrued
in their deft, precise researches—
"Hypothesize. Experiment. Conclude."

is one well-known example, or
"We die of the cold
and not of the darkness."—
are stamped in letters of electrum or gold

on the coins they lavish,
which the mind ceaselessly strokes
in its pitch-black hole.
"But seriously, folks,"

stop reading for a minute
and try to think about her.
She claims she hates words.
She lives alone in a condominium cluster,

shingled in cedar, its courtyards
defensible, its openings alarmed,
built just recently on land
where holsteins were once farmed.

Sometimes the alarms go off
in sequence or in chorus,
though no one's ever there.
Her dreams, too, she feels, are porous

in exactly the same way,
but since she likes guns
even less than talk, she fights
the invisible's unkillable invasions

with pyramids, intermetallic compounds,
zither music, authentic moon rocks,
and takes long particle baths
in the handmade orgone box

her ex had no room for
the day he jumped the fence.
One night she lay in a field
waiting for the harmonic convergence,

came home soaked and feverish
to throw the beef and pork
away, and clean and clean
until her house gleamed like a tuning fork.

Nothing ever came of that.
No footnotes care to mention
how her anger rusted to anguish.
But still she deserves a lifetime pension,

because, not being embittered
by the world's creepy so-and-sos,
no wave of malice has ever curled
over her, but it froze,

and never broke. So while I know
too well we should all regret
that she flutters through the meshes
of the world's iron information net,

why shouldn't we, to do her the justice
she deserves, ask ourselves if
one night she awakens,
cold and dazed, thirsty and stiff,

and sees, in shadows, an ad hoc committee
of murmurously chanting druids
calling for her sacrifice,
and swallows their concocted fluids,

could we, who write her down
for hours at a stretch,
lay our hands on her,
make her gag and retch,

though, when it comes to her body,
our knowledge compels restraint?
You tell me. "Rescued
from death by force though pale and faint."

Prothalamion

After telling the official in charge
of your surveillance that you won't make full
confessions, but you'll agree, nonetheless,
to sign below NO LONGER AT LARGE —
Send Pills From Now On To The Same Address,
you taxi home, amazed new owners of
something so sharply dialectical
you hardly know what else you're alive for
except to snarl, roped here, dangling above
its frantic, boiling core,
while stray dogs lick your feet, inspectors list
your damaged parts, whole families renew
their faith as they observe you spin,
and the price you pay for being you
doubles with every counterclockwise twist.
Such nameless terror, and don't I know it.
Such ancient terror, studded with foreign
instruments, freshly painted, retrofit
with missiles, lifts a robot arm to say:
Dear hearts, blessings will rain upon your heads;
your sheep will fatten, your children excel
in battle, insofar as you obey
and draw your water from this sacred well.
"What sheep?" you itch to ask. "What well?" although,
(and I'm not trying to be mean to you)
as slick as you've been, you are indeed
fallen for good now in the well of need,
mute, mummified in love and trust;
and if you back out now you just spoil the fun
for us, your friends who have a stake in you,
and leave yourselves half-bandaged on the rack.
And think of the gifts they'd make you give back:
the rhinestone inlaid bit and spur,
the strangely boring sex videotape.
Also, you have the future to consider,

from which, the word is, you won't escape.
The public notice of your stated intent
to take each other by the hands
and drown in its flowing element
is posted there in big red letters.
Read it and weep, and then conjure with
the Rosetta stone of your creation myth.

A Preservation Society Minute

The face is gone that pushed against the window
because the window's gone:
shattered by a paving stone.
The heaviest green summer can throw

across the manmade to cover its shame
curls over the unhinged doors,
creeps along the vacant floors.
Wasps nest in the very same

chink he laid his ear on when
the strangled sounds they made
left him feeling funny and afraid.
And you want to go back? Look again?

Buy the place? Restore it? Not a chance.
For now I'd rather skip
the joys of homeownership.
And as for that pile's marmoreal romance,

I tripped on that when a ghost whirled
around on me, to half-drown me
in his ruin's slipshod eternity,
who also once came from a smaller world

only to find, after hard travel,
only the cat alive and whole,
fat on hoppers and the occasional mole,
sleeping in the circumference of a well filled with gravel.

The Gulley

I heard two shots as I slipped out across
138th Street, where the city dives
from Sugar Hill's tangled elevations
to mix it up around the lives

that wring themselves out in crack dens, temples
of learning, social clubs, and cobbled mews,
or the hushed and spotless tulip precincts
with tulips opening on their avenues

and doormen huddled under April water.
Above me, startled from high tension wires,
birds split five ways over a neighborhood
lit like a bivouac by barrel fires,

which in turn mirrored the peach-tinted lights
I tried to shield off as I craned to see
the backlit, exaggerated figure,
the nominal son of the family.

This was his night to grow bug-eyed
and jump the groove to go trash and wreck
until the morning. One punctual scream
touched a small hair on the back of my neck

before omnidirectional silence,
serviceable, unthinking, superimposed
itself on all of us who straggled there.
A window opened, and then it was closed

and latched in a third-floor flat behind me.
That was my cue to walk away.
Each needle tracking a magnetic source
could have turned one shining head my way,

to force me down the gulley's glass-smooth walls,
though for now I was free, freed by the slim
off-chance that had smuggled me between
the man who fired and whatever made him.

Party Girl

She laughs, she cries, she turns, blinking, to squeeze
his hand on his knee, which then moves to hers.
From its wild intervals, the music confers
a length of feeling, like a robe of honor
custom-made to magnify these

twain, or so it must look, as gates of bronze
they've been scratching at forever by now
open, and, in a flash, translated from
our crapulous city's sizzle and hum,
they walk like one person on empty lawns;

the shaved acres of just-cut grass, the fast-
blooming orchids, the gold light that flails
the synesthesias of a voice so green
it has to be believed to be seen,
convince them the drama is here at last,

which, soon enough, will pilot them to bed.
But can this touching of theirs really make
the itching chords resolve? Or are they
about to be cut in half? Salome,
put to the sword for the love of a head,

could tell us which if she weren't so busy
backstage. The opera over, they exit
with four eyes fixed on the direct approach,
singing, "Bliss it was in that darkened coach . . ."
in the beat-up livery, off-tilt, dizzy

with the taste of supreme expectation
excruciatingly flavored by the tart
interrelationships of life and art.
But, oh, if what should happen does
a cry of love will fenestrate this nation,

and the millions, peeled of every defense,
will flood the presses with personal ads—
"Always lonely, but sick of fads;
likes animals, sunsets; please, no smokers;
is well-travelled and has experience."

"Let Me Play the Lion Too"

You or I could break a neck
better appointed to hang a necklace on
just from the strain of staring
inwardly at the low-tech,

age of bronze conflicts our mental parts
act out again and again.
In there, reduced in size,
a disgusted celestial being departs,

phalanxes pour fire, the trench
fills with the fallen, whose eyes
glitter and click; and *"Merde!"*
I'd say if I were French

as the dust blows off to reveal
wimpled shadows stripping
the dead and our champion with
an iconoclasm in his heel.

* * *

Gruesome though they are, these tight
claustral spaces do draw me in
to be the mere stem of myself
in battles I both document and fight;

but the inchwide mean streaks
I'm assigned to patrol,
from the gasping fissures of which
a mighty oracle speaks

of who we are and where we're heading,
leave you circumspect and cold.
You'd rather go out and make coalition
with the recklessness spreading

its chlorophyll through the morning glory.
Well I would too.
Let me play the lion too
and wear your skirts to tell your story

about someone burdened by an attitude
who threw his shield down and ran
from the mud and the wailing,
happily becoming unglued

in defeat, dead to this world but not yet
alive to the next, until
he stopped at a puncheon bridge
in a forest where three streams met

and stood there waiting for a few
tense minutes, to watch
a hawk in flight, and then
he crossed that bridge as I cross to you.

Beginner

When I remembered that I could see
I knew which way to look
to find the generic tree:
one fanged root steeping in a brook,

one branch the backsliding earth.
Real bark, purple finches, real gold leaf,
and, for what it was worth,
voices decent with grief

kept struggling to assert
and explain themselves.
I'd have given the shirt
off my back and emptied my shelves

of my choicest inventory
to have left that dark but growing place
before I'd heard the rest of their story
or been called to face

that life they thought would keep them sane:
rooted there like a lightning rod
eagerly anticipating rain,
scrimshawed

with warning in every human script
to remind whoever cared
that its price was pure Egypt,
and only by paying would their days be spared.

3

from *An Oral History of Migration*

Back in 1935 the Lord
told me, Go buy a guitar.
You be that thing, He said.
It was 6:47, almost 7:00 A.M.
The nettles and blackberry
I'd cut back the last spring
were already rooting at the stile
and bothering the chicken fence.
I was shoeing the team in the shed.
My mother called from deep in the yard:
"Run bring me a pail," she said.
Well, you can't fetch light with a pail,
at least not our pail,
so I pretended not to hear
and kept on working.
I was good shoeing horses, I'd
rasp and trim every hoof first,
then go around and drive the half-flat nails
flat side out into shoe and hoof
with a double stroke a little like a banjo lick.
But not too deep
or you drive to the quick.
You be that thing, He said.

Some people think if you keep jumping
over a patch of ground, jump
like some bighorn sheep,
that patch of ground eventually go away.
It don't; it's always there.
Up in Harlem after the war I quit the shipyards,
got myself a Gibson and a little reputation.
I've been turning it over ever since.

The Lump

I was in the gaffing hatch
tying spreads of salmon gear
with a box of No. 2 hooks, a spool
of sixty-pound-test monofilament leader,

assorted plugs, spoons, and baiters—
red and copper spoons, wooden
plugs with painted eyes, E-Z
baiters I'd rig with the carcasses

of six-inch herring for the big king salmon
that graze the deepwater commons
of the seamounts and offshore reefs.
They were there to be taken,

and from Mendocino north to Canada
we'd been taking for weeks—
the one thousand antique
two-poled trolling boats

of the Oregon, Washington, California fleets
fanned out like trace hounds
on the liquid furrows
to hunt the king salmon

the Five Tribes once worshipped.
That season we were enjoying
the best harvest in a generation.
The bankers were happy,

the bartenders were happy,
and the hookers who flew in
from Reno and Portland
grinned unceasingly on every corner

of every bayfront on the humming coast.
But I was content just to
grin back, since I was involved
and, of course, we were planning

to leave the ocean for a place less scenic.
I said Rajasthan, she said Sahara,
but we knew beyond question
it was desert we were after

the minute I saved eight thousand dollars.
Eight thousand dollars
(which I imagined stacked
in eight thousand one-dollar bills)

would get us out of the wind
falling that day in sheets
from a sky rubbed albino white
and watering with static

down to a cloth-of-silver bay
palisaded by the hundred idling masts
of a bottled-up fleet
spinning slowly on its anchor chains

in frustration. Because that week
no boat was fishing.
There was a lump on the ocean
that no fisherman would try.

A ridge of high pressure coiled and uncoiled
from the Gulf of Alaska
to the Sea of Japan:
a solid wall of running weather

disappearing into space,
which the sun every morning
would peel dry of moisture
and stretch taut

and start drumming with a rhythm
the Pacific had been turning to
since time out of mind.
And down along the trench of silver

the noontime sun dug to the horizon
you could watch the lump form.
A saw-toothed running swell,
blowing off at the edges,

would break the ocean's luminous skin
in simultaneous explosions,
glittering with malice, beautiful
from a distance, and announce

a relentless northwester's arrival —
churning and blowing
until night fell,
as the days slackened to equinox,

clearing the ocean of all but the reckless,
or those clumsy giants,
tankers and freighters
that take five miles to make a turn.

* * *

Every year just this kind of weather
settles over the North Pacific
from July onwards,
causing, among other things,

the famous fogs of San Francisco Bay,
heat and drought inland, in
the central valleys and the mountains,
inadvertent conflagrations

on the recently logged-out units
of the fir and redwood Coast Range,
where a Forest Service worker,
dripping jellied fire from a cannister

strapped to his back to burn out
the alder brakes, salmonberry,
and miscellaneous brush from a stripped hillside,
to prepare it for planting,

can find himself, before he knows it,
stranded in a whipping brushfire.
And out on the ocean, even
in hours that are accidentally calm,

the feed scatters and the salmon lie down
and can't be fished.
Which explains why I was puzzled
when I noticed,

while storing away the spreads
of gear, the box of hooks,
the plugs, spoons, and baiters,
the crimpers and the pliers,

so I could go back home once again
and spend another evening
resting and anticipating,
hoping the weather would break,

that the boat usually moored in the slip
next to ours
was loading supplies
for what looked like a good ten-day trip.

Like our own, she was another
of the ancient
double-ended wooden trollers
built in Alaska near the turn of the century.

She was worked by a man and a woman,
with a dog to keep them company.
I'd talked to the woman once or twice—
we'd had exchanges, detached and laconic,

that anyone familiar with boats and docks
would immediately recognize.
I'd have to say that she was someone
I wouldn't have been able to fish with:

intense, attenuated, all edge
and no middle, too controlling,
as it seemed to me then,
for the warped space of a thirty-six-footer.

The dog, though, was sedate and polite.
I liked him and fed him often.
I don't remember now if
I'd ever talked to the man before that evening

but I went around then to ask him,
as casually as I could—
because I didn't want to jinx him—
if something had changed in the weather

that made them decide to try it.
He said no, not for three more days,
but that they were going anyway
to prospect on the Banks

and catch the odd fish in the mornings
before the ocean grew sloppy.
The boat was tough enough,
and they'd seen fronts like this before.

Afternoons they'd shut down
and nose into the swell.
Mornings they'd fish a little
and evenings look around,

and when the wind finally dropped
they'd be on top of the school
a day ahead of the fleet.
The lump wasn't so big to kick them over.

Because I'd heard about him that
he was circumspect and farsighted,
and also because I had no right to,
I didn't disagree; but, instead,

since I knew they'd had difficulties
during some of the best fishing—
a bent shaft, and then
a cracked prop, both requiring

expensive haulouts
while everyone else was making money—
I offered to show him where we fished,
and the gear we were using.

So I bisected a point on the charts
where we'd found a ball of feed
surging with herring and baby hake,
and told him that we followed it for days,

combing the deepwater fissures,
drilling our lines
through the boiling rips
from eighty fathoms out

to the never-seen mountains
with three port wires, three
starboard wires, two dog wires
on the bow, eight spreads

on every wire catching so many fish
we couldn't stop to clean them
and had to lay them on deck
wrapped in shrouds of wet burlap

so the sun wouldn't manhandle
the silver of their skins.
And then, when it started getting dark,
before the last pull of the wires,

we'd rip out their gills
along the gill rakers,
slit them lengthwise, gut
and scrape with a spoon the bloodlines

that wander their spines, pack
their bellies with flakes
of milk white, blue-edged ice,
lay them out in the bins

on a bed of ice, feed
the slick jewels we found inside
to pig-eyed gulls and whiskered seals,
and then pull the wires the last time.

And on that last pull,
with the coal-dark ocean poised
on the interwoven rim of twilight,
we saw, regularly,

a king salmonfish, radiating,
jump for a hook like the moon.
I wanted the same for them,
and I told them so,

and then I hopped on my bicycle
to go eat dinner over the bridge,
where I stopped for a while
to watch their boat crossing the bar

as the fog came spilling through
the broken dish of the bay
and tried to douse
the quilled lights of the harbor,

the many-colored lights of the harbor.
And I thought then, not
for the first, but, I suppose,
almost the last time,

that living outside history was best,
and that at moments like this, here,
in Oregon, I'd made it, free
and clear, standing like this

to watch a fishing boat
strobing down the line of buoys
past the No. 2 can,
the whistling can and guardian of the harbor.

* * *

A month passed before I found out
what eventually happened to them.
He was right; the wind
stood down three days later,

and all the boats in the fleet
ran up to Neah Bay,
grounds that from Oregon
we called the end of the world,

to fish the white-fleshed kings
that run the Frazer River.
When I came back I heard
that a dory fisherman working

the thirty-fathom line
had almost had the bow
of his dory knocked off
by their double-ender

running straight east for the beach.
He yelled from his hatch,
"You son of a bitch,"
and then looked closer

and went over to his radio
to call the Coast Guard,
who sent their forty-footer out quickly
and retrieved the boat

just before it racked up on the reefs.
The yeoman who entered
the wheelhouse, to check out
the charm bracelet, the lucky doorknob,

the pictures and postcards
from a friend in Paris,
the 8-by-12 reproduction
of a unicorn tapestry tacked

above the compass, found the dog
sleeping quietly in the fo'c'sle.
The couple had vanished.
They speculate,

because the gear was trailing
with a few drowned salmon
hanging on the spreads,
that one morning they found the school

and kept fishing as the wind came up,
and that she, while going
up to the galley, or at the scuppers
tying down a stabilizer,

was bucked into the water
by a rogue swell,
and that he jumped in after her
to try to save her

from the always funnelling currents
that take a body down
instantaneously.
Others suggest that he was the one

who went in first, losing
his footing on the rolling deck,
and that she was the one who followed
to rescue him.

But what the public explanations,
consistent as they are
with the facts we have, don't explain,
and what mystifies me still,

even though I think about them
not often but regularly,
is why neither one put
the boat in idle when he or she went after

whichever one went overboard.
The boat kept on moving
in a fast troll, made
thirty miles and almost swamped

a dory in its passion for land.
What I would have done
is throttle down the boat
and then go in

sure of a place to swim back to
win or lose.
Given that neither were amateurs,
why didn't they do that, too?

And the darker theories, the ones
that address their obvious desperation,
though they have their attractions,
seem wrong, seem unsatisfying to me.

For all we know, they might have been
transported somewhere.
And what about the dog,
an animal they loved, who,

thanks to the Coast Guard,
now lives with a family in Waldport,
a town on the Alsea River
fifteen miles from where we were.

Lifeline

As soon as he realized he was lost, that
in kicking around his new job in his head,
the new people he'd met, and how
he could manage a week in Seaside,
he'd stumbled past the muddy fork of road
that slithered down in switchbacks
to Highway 20, and now couldn't tell,
through rainclouds coarse as pig iron,
and about as cold, which languished
over each of the scarred mountaintops,
where west was, or east, or north,
or feel the sun's direction,
he stopped, as he knew he should,
and doubled back. An hour at the worst
would bring him to the International
inert in a ditch with its radiator
punctured, its axle broken, and blood
from his temple on the steering wheel.
He wished he'd never set eyes on that truck . . .
here he was, trudging like an idiot
through a thousand-square-mile dead spot
of Douglas fir, soaked to the bone
and hungry, with his head throbbing.
He wasn't up to this, he said to himself,
staring disconsolately outward
to the numberless ridges and valleys, singed
with the bitter green of the firs.
But why hadn't he reached the truck yet,
or at least somewhere familiar,
where he could get his bearings again?
He didn't recognize the ridge he was on.
He'd never seen this particular patch—
glinting with wild crocus prongs—
of clear-cut ground, torched and scarified.
Should he keep going, or return again?

There and then he made his third mistake.
Hearing, or thinking he heard,
deep in the valley below him plunged
in mist, a chain saw start and sputter,
he made off down toward the sound.
It would be a gypo logger, scrounging
deadfall cedar for shake-bolt cords,
or a civilian with a twenty-dollar permit
to cut firewood for sale at a roadside stand.
Either way, he could get directions
and hitch home by dark. Hours later,
night found him in a hollow, shouting
until he was hoarse for someone, anyone.
The weekend was almost here, and no one
at work would miss him before Monday . . .
he lived alone, idiot, he lived alone
and couldn't count on a single person ·
to send out an alarm. Those first hours
he spent shivering under a lip of rock,
wide awake, startling at each furtive,
night-hunting animal sound, each flap
of the raptors in the branches overhead.
On the second day he lost his glasses.
It happened like this: As he struggled
over the cryptic terrain all morning —
terrain that would seem, if looked at
from high above, from a helicopter
or a plane flying low enough to pierce
the dense, lazy foliage of clouds,
created, finessed, meticulously contrived
to amaze, like a marvellous relief map
of papier-mâché, revealing its artifice only
in the improbable dramas of its contours,
its extravagant, unlikely colors —
he had what amounted to a real insight.
All this was the brainchild of water.
Stretching back beyond the Pleistocene —
how many millions of years? —
imperial rain had traced without pity,

over and over again, its counterimage
on the newborn, jagged mountains
until the length of the coast had been
disciplined to a system designed
to irrigate and to nourish the soil.
He decided he'd follow the water down.
He'd use each widening tributary
like the rung of a ladder, to climb down
from his awful predicament, and soon
work his way to the ocean—though, of course,
long before that he'd run across people.
With this in mind, he came to a stream
heavy and brown with the spring runoff,
its embankment on his side steep
to the point of perpendicularity, thick
with brush, though on the other side
a crown of ferns tumbled gently down
to the next watershed. It seemed like
a good idea to cross, and farther on
he found a logged fir with a choker cable
still attached (it must have snapped
when they tried to yard the falled tree
to the road high above) straddling
the stream. A little more than halfway over
he slipped on the treacherous wood
and would have gone in but for the cable,
which he lunged at just in time.
That was his lifeline, though flailing
to save himself, he knocked the glasses
from his head. Now they'd reach the sea
long before him, if he ever would.
He knelt down in the ferns, exhausted,
by fits growing determined never
to leave that spot. They'd find his bones
fifty years from now, clothes and ID
rotted away, a trillium poking through
his ribcage, a cucumber vine trellised
by the seven sockets in his skull.
The play of the thin, unending drizzle

on the overlapping leaves he sank below,
on the bark of the impassive trees
looming around him, grew indistinguishable
from the pulse turning loud in his head.
The bruise on his forehead throbbed.
There were rents and gashes everywhere
down the length of his rain gear, which
let the mist and the dampness in.
Beyond a scant dozen inches, the world
looked blurry, smeared bright, unattainable.
Nothing in his life, up until then
(and if this had been pointed out to him
he would have acknowledged pride in it),
suggested that anything resembling
a speculative turn of mind cannibalized
the adequate, rhythmic, progressive
movements of his thoughts and feelings.
But, still, as almost everyone does,
he'd occasionally had inklings, stirrings,
promptings, and strange intuitions
about something just beyond the radius
of his life — not divine, necessarily,
but what people meant when they referred
to such things — which gave to the least
of his actions its dream of complicity.
Now he recognized, with a shock
almost physical, that those inklings
were just the returning, reanimated echo
(on a different scale but similar
to the echo we sometimes hear in our skulls,
which leads us to the uncanny feeling
that an experience we're having is one
we've had before, at some other time —
but does anything ever repeat itself?)
of the vibrations his life made
bouncing off the things around him
sunk deep in their own being;
and that life, his life, blossoming now
in this daisy chain of accident and error,

was nothing more or less than what there was.
There was nothing hidden underneath this,
but it was small, so small, as the life
of his family was, his people, his species
among the other species—firs, owls,
plants whose names he didn't know—
all of them minute, and the earth itself,
its four billion plus years of life
just the faint, phosphorescent track
of a minute sea creature on an ocean
for the annihilating dimensions of which
words such as "infinite" and "eternal"
were ridiculous in their inadequacy.
He lay on his back inside the ferns
and listened to the rain's clepsydral ticking.
He tried to grasp—what was it?—
but it clattered away, that slight change
in the pressure binding thing to thing,
as when an upright sleeper shifts
just a little, imparting to his dreams
an entirely different train of meaning.
Beyond those clouds, the blue was there
which shaded to blackness, and beyond
that blackness the uncounted, terrifying
celestial entities hung suspended only
by the influence they had on one another.
And all of this was just a seed
inside a seed inside a seed. . . .
So that when, finally, late the next morning
he half-crawled out of the woods, and came
in time to a wire fence in a clearing,
less than two feet high and decorated
with gleaming ceramic insulators,
which indicated that a mild current,
five volts at the most, ran through it
to keep the foraging animals off
the newly sown vegetable garden
enclosed inside its perimeter, and saw
beyond it the sprawl of the lawn,

the 4-by-4 parked in the driveway,
the Stars and Stripes on the flagpole,
and the house, he stopped, paralyzed.
The wind was blowing northwest, the clouds
were breaking up under its steady persuasion,
but, try as he did, he couldn't will
himself to step lightly over that wire,
and cross the garden's sweet geometry,
and go up to the door and ask to be
fed and made warm and taken home.
By that small fence, he sat down and wept.

VIJAY SESHADRI was born in India and came to America at age five. He grew up in Columbus, Ohio. His work has appeared in the *Threepenny Review*, the *New Yorker*, *Shenandoah*, *Antaeus*, *AGNI*, and the *Paris Review*. He currently lives in Brooklyn.

This book was designed by Will Powers. It is set in Joanna type and manufactured by BookMobile Design and Publishing Services on acid-free paper. Cover design by Jeenee Lee.